Remembering Sacramento

James Scott and Tom Tolley

TURNER
PUBLISHING COMPANY

The downtown streets of a bygone Sacramento come alive with pedestrians, streetcars, and the automobile.

Remembering
Sacramento

Turner Publishing Company
Remembering Sacramento

www.turnerpublishing.com

Copyright © 2010 Turner Publishing Company

Library of Congress Control Number: 2010923498

ISBN: 978-1-59652-628-0

Printed in the United States of America

ISBN 978-1-68336-880-9 (hc)

CONTENTS

An unusual scene of a horse-drawn buggy on the streets of Sacramento well into the established automobile era.

ACKNOWLEDGMENTS

This volume, *Remembering Sacramento,* is the result of the cooperation and efforts of one exclusive archive. It is with great thanks that we acknowledge the valuable contribution of the Sacramento Archives and Museum Collection Center.

We would also like to thank James Scott and Tom Tolley for valuable contributions and assistance in making this work possible.

PREFACE

Sacramento has thousands of historic photographs that reside in archives, both locally and nationally. This book began with the observation that, while those photographs are of great interest to many, they are not easily accessible. During a time when Sacramento is looking ahead and evaluating its future course, many people are asking, How do we treat the past? These decisions affect every aspect of the city—architecture, public spaces, commerce, infrastructure—and these, in turn, affect the way that people live their lives. This book seeks to provide easy access to a valuable, objective look into the history of Sacramento.

The power of photographs is that they are less subjective than words in their treatment of history. Although the photographer can make subjective decisions regarding subject matter and how to capture and present it, photographs seldom interpret the past to the extent textual histories can. For this reason, photography is uniquely positioned to offer an original, untainted look at the past, allowing the viewer to learn for himself what the world was like a century or more ago.

This project represents countless hours of review and research. The researchers and writers have reviewed thousands of photographs in numerous archives. We greatly appreciate the generous assistance of the individuals and organizations listed in the acknowledgments of this work, without whom this project could not have been completed.

The goal in publishing this work is to provide broader access to this set of extraordinary photographs that seek to inspire, provide perspective, and evoke insight that might assist people who are responsible for determining Sacramento's future. In addition, the book seeks to preserve the past with adequate respect and reverence.

With the exception of touching up imperfections that have accrued with the passage of time and cropping where necessary, no changes have been made. The focus and clarity of many images are limited to the technology and the ability of the photographer at the time they were recorded.

The work is divided into eras. Beginning with some of the earliest known photographs of Sacramento, the first section records photographs through the end of the nineteenth century. The second section spans the beginning of the twentieth century to the World War I era. Section Three moves into the period between the wars. The last section takes a look at the World War II and postwar eras up to 1960. In each of these sections we have made an effort to capture various aspects of life through our selection of photographs. People, commerce, transportation, infrastructure, religious institutions, and educational institutions have been included to provide a broad perspective.

We encourage readers to reflect as they go walking in Sacramento, strolling through the city, its parks, and its neighborhoods. It is the publisher's hope that in utilizing this work, longtime residents will learn something new and that new residents will gain a perspective on where Sacramento has been, so that each can contribute to its future.

—Todd Bottorff, Publisher

Central Pacific Railroad Depot (ca. 1882).

In the Right Place, at the Right Time

(1860s–1899)

Post Office near St. Rose Square (ca. 1890).

The Leonard Kellogg
Hardware Store (ca. 1883).

Wells Fargo Express Building on 2nd Street.

Sacramento County Courthouse on 7th Street (ca. 1865). This second Sacramento courthouse was built in 1855, and it served as a meeting place for the state legislature until the state capitol was completed in 1869.

Electric streetcar in downtown Sacramento (ca. 1891).

Horse auction at 3rd and J streets (ca. 1879).

Streetcars in Oak Park at the turn of the century.

Breuner's Furniture Building (late 1800s).

Sacramento's first jail, in service from 1850 until 1861, the Sacramento River, and H Street (ca. 1860).

Mechanics' Store on K Street (ca. 1878).

Old Wayside Bar (ca. 1890).

Chinese parade along the Southern Pacific Railroad tracks.

Sacramento County Courthouse
(4th of July, 1907).

Gaining Stride

(1900–1917)

J Street shops (ca. 1910).

John Breuner Company at 6th and K streets (ca. 1900).

California National Bank at J
and 4th streets (ca. 1910).

Sacramento Gas and Electric Railway Company Station "A" Building, at 6th and H streets (ca. 1904).

Sacramento Gas and Electric Railway Company Car Barn at 28th Street between M and N streets (ca. 1904).

Southern Pacific (previously Central) Depot at I Street (ca. 1904).

The rubble of Weinstock's Store at 4th and K streets after a fire (ca. 1903).

Fire engine in a parade at J Street (ca. 1916).

Fire Department Engine Company in downtown Sacramento.

A view of J Street (ca. 1909).

View of K and 8th streets (ca. 1912). United Cigars and the Ambrosia Cafeteria are visible.

The California State Capitol
(ca. 1910).

St. Francis Church at L Street (ca. 1911).

Businesses on J Street (ca. 1915).

A view of J Street (ca. 1912).

Peerless Ice Cream wagon in a parade at J Street (ca. 1916).

A Capital City Wheelmen Club race at the agricultural park (ca. 1900).

View of the racetrack at the "Sacramento Day" parade (ca. 1909).

Ruhstaller's Steam Beer advertising sign at the Sacramento street fair (1904 or 1905).

Train engine entertainment at the California state fair (ca. 1917). Trouble was, the engines could perform for one show only.

A delivery wagon carries Buffalo Brewery beer kegs at 12th and H streets at the I Street bridge.

Street scene at J Street.

The "Wells Fargo & Co. Express, Denver and Rio Grande Express" at H Street (ca. 1900).

Joining the Nation

(1918–1939)

The Coca-Cola Bottling Company on Sacramento Boulevard (ca. 1928).

Cityscape of downtown Sacramento (ca. 1921).

Street scene at 10th and K streets (ca. 1925). Cathedral of the Blessed Sacrament and Mohr and Yoerk Market are visible to the left, the Hotel Sacramento to the right.

Post Office at 7th and K streets (ca. 1920).

View of the Fratt Building at the corner of 2nd and K streets (ca. 1928). The Standard Employment Agency, Pacific Drug Company, and Alaskan Rooms are visible.

Cityscape at 9th and K streets (ca. 1920). The State Capitol is visible to the left and capitol extension building (now the state library and courts building) is under construction to the right.

The California State Capitol
(ca. 1922).

The State Capitol and cityscape (ca. 1920).

Parade at K Street (ca. 1920). The Post Office and Eaglesons Clothing Store are visible.

Fire engine at L Street (ca. 1924).

Elks building at J and 11th streets (ca. 1928).

McCurry Company car fitted with a camera platform on 10th Street between I and J streets (ca. 1924). The Plaza Park and Western States Life Building is visible.

State fair harness races at Stockton Boulevard (ca. 1926).

The *Delta King* steamer on the Sacramento River during 4th of July festivities (ca. 1929).

Photo shoot in front of Red Cross offices at 8th Street (ca. 1924).

Charles Lindbergh speaks to Sacramento citizens (ca. 1927).

View of J Street (1929). The National Cash Register Company is visible.

Motorcycles advertise the Harley-Davidson Store on J Street (ca. 1924).

A view of 10th Street (ca. 1929).
The restaurant sign says "Oysters,
Nick Never Sleeps."

The State Library and Courts building in the capitol extension group (ca. 1920). On the architrave are the words "Into the Highlands of the Mind Let Me Go."

Shown here is the Tim Anspach Mule Company stagecoach at 30th and R streets (ca. 1925).

Sacramento Northern Railroad Cars at 8th and K streets (ca. 1925). The train ran from Chico to Sacramento to San Francisco in the 1920s and 1930s, and was the longest interurban electric line in the U.S. (229 miles). Ambrosia Cafeteria is visible to the far left.

Racing car (1920s).

Street scene at 12th and J streets (ca. 1925). Elks Building and State Theatre are visible to the right and the California Life Building to the left.

Street scene at 8th and K streets (ca. 1920). The Hotel Clunie and Bergman's Hats are visible to the left.

Night view of 10th and K streets (ca. 1920). The Sutter Restaurant is visible to the right and Levinsons Bookstore and Hotel Land to the left.

View of J Street (ca. 1922). The Bank of Italy (later the Bank of America) is visible in foreground to the right.

The Osborn and Folger Ice Company on I Street.

Business on L Street halts to pose for the camera.

California State Life Insurance Building (ca. 1928).

Western Hotel at 3rd and K streets (ca. 1931).

Ben Ali Shriners bands parade down J Street (ca. 1937). Among other businesses, Coast Radio is visible in the Ruhstaller Building, at right.

Hotel Sacramento at the northwest corner of 10th and K streets (ca. 1930).

State Theatre at 12th and J streets (ca. 1924).

View of J Street (ca. 1926). State Theater and Elks Club are visible to the right and California Life Building to the left.

A marching band participates in the opening of Tower Bridge (ca. 1935).

View of K Street.

The National Bank of D. O. Mills at 7th and J streets is visible in this rooftop view (ca. 1925).

The Sacramento Solons Baseball Team at Edmond's Field (ca. 1935).

Downtown Sacramento (ca. 1939). The tower of the Church of the Blessed Sacrament is visible in front of the Elks Club tower.

Aerial view of the State Capitol and the surrounding downtown area (ca. 1930).

A view of J and Front streets (ca. 1931). Businesses include Square Deal Clothing Store, Western Labor Agency, and the Wheel Hotel.

Downtown Sacramento (ca. 1938).

The E. W. Myers Jewelry Store on K Street, with signs for the California Beauty College located upstairs (ca. 1931).

Capitol Theater at K Street (ca. 1937).

View of K Street (ca. 1920). Hotel Land and Hotel Sacramento are visible to the right.

K Street (ca. 1927).

The Mebius and Drescher Company Wholesale Grocers building, at the southeast corner of Front and K streets (ca. 1931).

A view of K Street (ca. 1938). The Flying Eagle Cafe, Capitol Loan, Rialto Theater, and the Equipoise Cigar Shop are visible.

Western Hotel and other businesses at K Street (ca. 1937).

The aviator "Wrong Way" Corrigan in a convertible California Highway Patrol car (ca. 1938).

K Street (ca. 1931). Hotel Land, the Sutter Restaurant, Hotel Sacramento, and the Hippodrome are visible.

View of K Street (ca. 1931). Visible businesses include Hale Brothers, the Owl Drug Company, and Albert Elkus.

View of Firehouse no. 4 at 5th Street (ca. 1938). Lun's Laundry is next door and Capitol City Plating Works behind.

Pony Express historic marker (ca. 1938).

Streetcar at 7th and K streets with the Post Office in the background (ca. 1930).

Front gate of Sutter's Fort
at L Street (ca. 1939).

View of K Street (late 1930s).

View of K and 10th streets.

The S. H. Kress and Company and Montgomery Ward stores are visible among other businesses in this view of K Street (late 1930s).

A view of 10th and L streets. Mission Orange Coffee Shop and Red Heart Pastry Shop are visible at the corner, Hotel Land in the distance.

Facing the Future

(1940–1960)

The *Spirit of St. Louis* is on display during a visit by Charles Lindbergh to Mather Field.

A view of 4th and M streets (ca. 1942).

Alhambra Theatre at 31st Street and Alhambra Boulevard (ca. 1940).

Pedestrians brave snow-covered sidewalks on 9th and K streets (ca. 1942).

Western Pacific Railroad tracks near the depot on J Street (ca. 1940).

Fire at El Rey
Theater at J Street
(ca. 1941).

Fire fighters struggle to contain the El Rey Theater blaze.

Removal of streetcar tracks at 10th and K streets (ca. 1948).

Demolished tracks at 10th and K streets (ca. 1948).

Admission Day parade at K Street (ca. 1940).

Mercy Hospital at J Street (ca. 1942).

View of 3rd and K streets.

View of 9th and K streets (ca. 1945).

An aerial view of Sacramento downtown (early 1940s).

View of 4th and M streets (ca. 1942).

View of 4th and M streets (ca. 1942).

View of 9th and K streets (ca. 1942).

President Harry Truman at the Southern Pacific Depot (ca. 1948).

Cathedral of the Blessed Sacrament
at 11th and K streets (ca. 1949).

As capital of the
"Golden State,"
Sacramento is home
to the magnificent
State Capitol
(ca. 1960).

Sacramento Municipal Airport under construction at Freeport Boulevard (ca. 1954).

Southern Pacific Depot (ca. 1955).

A political campaign parade with Governor Adlai Stevenson in an open car at K Street (ca. 1955). Weinstock Department Store and Sears Roebuck and Company are visible in the background.

Veterans Memorial Service by the Madres de la Guerra at the Mexican Center at 6th Street (ca. 1954). In the background is a partial view of the Tony Beretta Club.

Parade at J Street (ca. 1950).

Entrance to Capitol Park at 10th and L streets (ca. 1952).

The governor's mansion (originally the Albert Gallatin House) at 16th and H streets.

A crowd forms in front of Weinstock's Department Store.

Scottish Rite Temple at L Street (ca. 1950).

An aerial view of Sacramento as it looked around 1960.

Notes on the Photographs

These notes, listed by page number, attempt to include all aspects known of the photographs. Each of the photographs is identified by the page number, a title or description, photographer and collection, archive, and call or box number when applicable. Although every attempt was made to collect all data, in some cases complete data may have been unavailable due to the age and condition of some of the photographs and records.

Printed in the USA
CPSIA information can be obtained
at www.ICGtesting.com
JSHW072025140824
68134JS00042B/3794